WHERE PEOPLE LIVE

Living at
the Coast

Neil Morris

A⁺

Smart Apple Media

Published by Smart Apple Media
2140 Howard Drive West, North Mankato, Minnesota 56003

Designed by Helen James

Photographs by Corbis (AFP, Paul Almasy, Dave Bartruff, Nathan Benn, Richard Bickel, Jonathan Blair, Michael Busselle, Pablo Corral V, Richard Cummins, Natalie Fobes, Gunter Marx Photography, Nick Hawkes; Ecoscene, Lindsay Hebberd, Jeremy Horner, Dave G. Houser, Hulton-Deutsch Collection, Hanan Isachar, Attar Maher/Corbis Sygma, James Marshall, Charles O'Rear, Gianni Dagli Orti, Carl & Ann Purcell, Reuters NewMedia Inc., Bill Ross, Royalty-Free, Michael T. Sedam, ML Sinibaldi, Paul A. Souders, Tim Thompson, Peter Turnley, Penny Tweedie, Patrick Ward, Staffan Widstrand, Roger Wood, Michael S. Yamashita)

Printed in the United States of America

Library of Congress Cataloging-in-Publication Data

Morris, Neil.
Living at the coast / by Neil Morris.
p. cm. — (Where people live)
Includes index.
Contents: Early settlement — Towns and cities — People of the coast — Ships and ports — Fishing — Natural hazards — Controlling the coast — Reclaiming the land — The frozen north — Tourist resorts — Using the coast — Pollution and conservation.
ISBN 1-58340-486-4
1. Ocean—Juvenile literature. 2. Coasts—Juvenile literature. 3. Coastal ecology—Juvenile literature.
[1. Coasts. 2. Coastal ecology. 3. Ecology.] I. Title.

GN386.M67 2004
909.0946—dc22   2003067296

First Edition

9 8 7 6 5 4 3 2 1

Contents

Introduction

In the past, many people chose to live on the coast because this location offered them the benefits of both land and sea. Coast-dwellers have always had a ready source of food waiting to be caught—fish. And since the development of ocean-going ships, they have also had the advantage of easy travel and trade. In earlier times, before the invention of trains or cars, boats were the most useful means of getting around. In more recent times, many people have chosen to make their homes beside the sea simply because the coast is a pleasant, interesting place to live. They are joined every year by vacationers, who flock to the seaside to relax and have fun.

▲ *The coastal waters of Alaska contain abundant salmon, halibut, cod, herring, pollack, shrimp, clams, and crabs—all contributing to the survival of coastal villages.*

Different coastlines

There are many different kinds of coasts. Some are rocky, with steep cliffs. Other shorelines have beautiful beaches, with **sand dunes** piled up behind them. People have had to **adapt** to these different conditions. In all cases, however, people of the coast have learned that living near the sea can be dangerous. They set their houses well away from the high-**tide** line. Over time,

Many people enjoy days at the seaside in beach huts such as these.

however, the sea may wear rocks away and come in farther, causing people to lose their homes. Many people would like to live in a house on the beach, but it might not be there for very long!

Exploring the world

When people used ships to explore the world and discover new lands, they generally sailed close to land. Some coasts became known as dangerous places, beyond which the world was unknown. This was the case with the **cape** at the southern tip of Africa, which Portuguese explorer Bartolomeu Dias discovered in 1488 and named the "Cape of Storms." But his king renamed it the "Cape of Good Hope," because he thought the route around it might lead to India—and all of its riches. He was soon proved right, and in 1498, the Cape was rounded. In 1652, Dutch traders who sailed the route landed and founded a settlement a little way up the coast. This grew into the modern city of Cape Town.

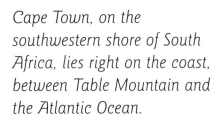

Cape Town, on the southwestern shore of South Africa, lies right on the coast, between Table Mountain and the Atlantic Ocean.

Early Settlement

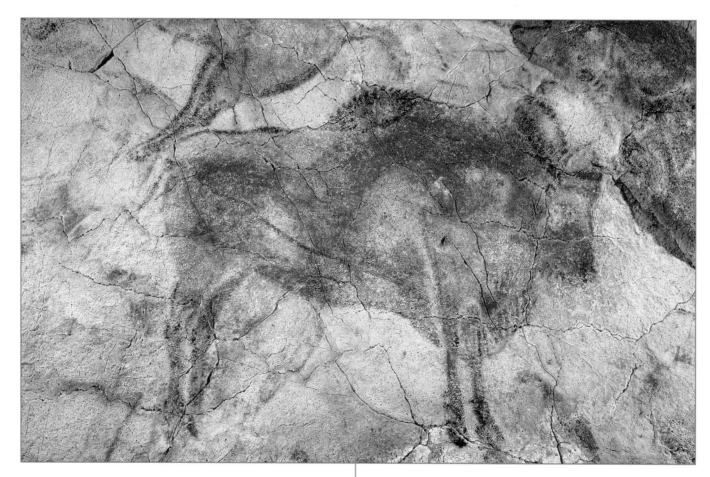

Historians believe that modern humans first appeared a very long time ago in Africa. About 100,000 years ago, groups of them began making their way into Asia. These early people were hunter-gatherers. As they moved around, they hunted wild animals and gathered fruit, berries, and roots for food. Many of them traveled along the coast because there they could catch fish, gather shellfish, and hunt other sea creatures, such as turtles. By 40,000 years ago, some groups of hunter-gatherers had reached Southeast Asia. Later, other groups crossed from northern Asia to North and then South America. In this way, people spread throughout the world, and many decided to settle along the coastlines.

▲ *Humans had reached Europe by 40,000 years ago. As in other parts of the world, some people sheltered in caves near the coast. These* **prehistoric** *paintings were made on the walls of a cave near the coast of northern Spain.*

Arnhem Land

Humans reached Australia from Southeast Asia, using boats to cross narrow strips of water. Around 40,000 years ago there was no sea between the large island of New Guinea and Australia—they formed one land mass—so the

Aborigines in Arnhem Land use elaborate songs and dramatic dances in their traditional celebrations.

coastline was different than it is today. Near the present northern coast of Australia, in a region called Arnhem Land, the first humans to arrive made many settlements. These people were the Aborigines (meaning "original inhabitants"), and thousands of them still live in the area. Their lands were named much more recently, after a Dutch explorer's ship (the *Arnhem*).

Coastal pyramids

Later, people realized that settlements on the coast gave them another advantage—they could see others coming. Some time after A.D. 1200, the Maya built a fortified settlement at Tulum, in the Yucatan Peninsula of Mexico. The buildings were on top of a cliff overlooking the Caribbean Sea. In 1518, a Spanish explorer saw the temple pyramids from his ship and was amazed at their size and beauty. He sailed past, but it was not long before Spanish conquerors had destroyed the Mayan civilization. Fortunately, the cliff-top ruins remain today.

The ruins of Tulum, overlooking the Caribbean Sea. Today, this stretch of coast is very popular with vacationers.

7

Towns and Cities

Over the centuries, many coastal settlements grew into villages and then gradually into towns. Trade was important to these towns, and many developed into major **ports**. In some cases, the growth was very rapid. An example of this is Carthage, in present-day Tunisia, on the Mediterranean coast of North Africa. Carthage was founded in 814 B.C. by sailors from Tyre, an early coastal town in the region of Phoenicia. The Phoenicians named their African settlement Karthadasht (meaning "new city"), and it grew rapidly into a **city-state**. From there, Carthaginians could sail easily to the Mediterranean islands of Corsica,

▲ *Most of the remains at the modern town of Tyre (also called Sur) are from the period when it became part of the Roman empire.*

Sardinia, and Sicily. Today the site of ancient Carthage lies in a **suburb** of the modern city of Tunis.

Chan Chan

Around A.D. 800, South American people called the Chimu began building an empire along the coastal region of Peru that lies between the Andes Mountains and the Pacific Ocean. Their capital of Chan Chan, near the modern industrial city

The city of Chan Chan was made up of separate compounds, or enclosed areas, containing temples, workshops, and storerooms, as well as adobe houses.

of Trujillo, grew into a large city with up to 20,000 inhabitants. Chan Chan was full of craftworkers and traders, as well as farmers and fishermen, who lived in houses made of adobe (sun-dried clay). Around 1470, the Chimu empire was conquered by the Incas, who carried off their skilled workers.

San Francisco

Before the arrival of Europeans, Native Americans of the Costanoan tribe lived along the coast of present-day California. They lived in cone-shaped dwellings thatched with reeds, twigs, or bark. The Costanoans got much of their food from the sea, and their diet included fish, mussels, and seals. In 1595, a Portuguese explorer sailed into a Californian bay and named it *Puerto de San Francisco* ("Port of Saint Francis"). By the 18th century, a Spanish expedition had built a military fort there, and in 1849, the harbor was filled with ships. This interest was caused by the California gold rush. San Francisco grew quickly into a thriving city, which today has a population of 1.6 million and is visited by 3 million tourists every year.

People in prosperous American coastal cities often revived the ornate architectural style of Victorian England.

9

People of the Coast

Among groups of people who made the coast their home, traditions and customs were passed from generation to generation. Many of these developed from the sea, especially its great bounty—fish. Other traditions came from sea travel and coastal trade. Some coastal peoples realized that they could exchange their own goods—especially fish and salt—for materials that they lacked. Today, the way of life of coastal people is changing in most parts of the world. Modern ways are replacing traditional methods. Nevertheless, a great deal can be learned from people who know how to live in tune with their surroundings.

▲ *The modern city of Da Nang, in Vietnam, lies along the coast of the South China Sea. People of this region have always been sailors, fishermen, and rice-growers.*

The Coast Salish

Native Americans of the northwest Pacific coast fished for their livelihood. They hollowed canoes from tree trunks and used hooks, nets, spears, and clubs to catch fish. The Salish tribe lived along the coast near present-day Vancouver, Canada. Like other people in the region, they lived in large longhouses made of cedar wood. Several families lived in one house. A huge carved

The colorful totem poles in Stanley Park are a major attraction for visitors to Vancouver, Canada.

▶

post, called a totem pole, stood in front of the house. The pole was usually carved with the figures of animals from ancient legends. Today, many **descendants** of the Coast Salish use modern methods to continue their fishing tradition.

The Swahili

The word "Swahili," meaning "coast people," refers to a large group of people living along the east coast of Africa. Historians believe they are descended from Arab traders who sailed down the coast around 2,000 years ago, settled there, and gradually mixed with Bantu-speaking Africans. Some coastal villages grew into great commercial ports and Swahili city-states, including Kilwa, Mombasa, and Zanzibar. There the Swahili traded gold and ivory from the African interior for goods from Arabia and China. Today, the Swahili language is the national language of Kenya and Tanzania, as well as being widely spoken in Uganda and Congo.

▼ *The coastal people of Kenya rely heavily on their boats to help them gather food and transport goods.*

Ships and Ports

Ships and boats have carried people and their goods across the seas for at least 5,000 years. People traveled in ships to explore and discover new lands, to settle in new parts of the world, and to trade with others. Sheltered harbors were built beside many coastal settlements, and some of these grew into major ports, forming links across the world's oceans. This has meant that people who live in coastal regions have always been influenced by other cultures and ways of life. At the same time, shipbuilding cities and trading ports have been able to provide local people with work. In recent years, inland airports have created competition to coastal ports, but a great deal of cargo (bulk goods) is still carried by ship.

▲ *Spanish sailors founded the settlement of Buenos Aires in 1536. Today, it is the capital and largest city of Argentina, with a population of 11 million. The people of Buenos Aires are called porteños ("port dwellers").*

Hanseatic League

Trading cities and ports along the North and Baltic Sea coasts came together to protect their common interests in the 13th century. They formed the Hanseatic League, or Hansa (*Hansa* is an Old German word meaning "company"). Before long, all the larger German cities were in the League, including Lübeck, the city where important meetings were held. By 1400, there were 160 member towns across northern Europe. League members developed a system of commercial laws and sailed between their ports

This gate was the medieval entrance to the city of Lübeck, which lies near the mouth of the Trave River, on the Baltic Sea. The port was founded in 1143. Today it has a population of 210,000.

in sturdy trading ships called cogs, which could hold large amounts of cargo. The Hanseatic League lasted until 1669, when the last **assembly** was held in Lübeck.

Pusan

The large industrial city of Pusan is the biggest port in South Korea. Life has changed for many people of this coastal region over the last 50 years. During that time their country has become a modern industrial nation. The port at Pusan is divided in two. One section deals with large and small fishing boats, and fishing continues to be important to the local community, as it was long ago. The other, larger section of the port has grown into an enormous **container** terminal, where ocean-going ships can load and unload their cargoes. The South Koreans also build ships at Pusan, alongside other kinds of heavy industry.

The coastal city of Pusan is home to a successful ship building industry.

Fishing

ishing has always been an important way of life for many people living along the world's coasts. Fishing communities once used small boats and canoes, and most of their catch was taken in shallow waters near land. During the 20th century, however, many nations began using much larger ships, which were owned by commercial companies rather than individuals or families. In many parts of the world today, big companies send their ships to the richest fishing grounds, leaving local fishermen to earn a living near their home coast. This has led to overfishing in regions such as the North Atlantic, where **restrictions** have been placed on the kinds and amounts of fish that may be caught. These restrictions, and the competition from large companies, have made things very difficult for small, traditional fishing communities.

Grimsby

The port of Grimsby lies on the northeast coast of England, on the **estuary** of the Humber River. It became an important fishing port in 1856, when a large fish dock was built there. The town was linked to the rest of England, including London, by a new railway. A second dock was

▼ *These fishermen, off the coast of Sri Lanka, still use their own traditional methods.*

A third dock was built at Grimsby in 1934, making it a very important fishing port. Unfortunately, local fishermen today are being forced out by commercial boats.

opened 30 years later, and as the port grew, more and more local people became involved in fishing. They either went out on the fishing boats or worked at the docks. In recent years, however, new regulations have meant less fishing for small boats, and many local people have been forced to find other work. Grimsby has become a leading center for the processing of frozen food.

Fish farms

Some coastal people have learned how to control the conditions in which fish and shellfish are kept. This system of fish farming, called aquaculture, is practiced all over the world. The leading fish-farming nations are China and Japan. Fish such as sea bream and yellowtail are kept in

large pens near the coast, where they can be properly fed and protected from natural **predators**. Oysters and mussels are farmed on poles and ropes in sea ponds, making it much easier to collect them. Some oyster farmers start their farms by putting shells or tiles on the sea bottom, and young oysters attach themselves to these.

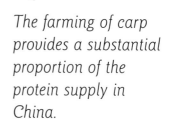

The farming of carp provides a substantial proportion of the protein supply in China.

Natural Hazards

People who choose to live near the coast know that they are in constant danger from the sea, especially during stormy weather. There is always the threat of flooding, and this threat could become worse if sea levels continue to rise. Scientists believe that temperatures around the world are gradually increasing, and that this global warming could increase the threat to coastlines. This is because the increase in temperature could melt some of the ice in the world's two polar regions, leading to an even greater rise in sea levels. In many parts of the world, people put up defenses such as walls and fences to try to save their coast. In places such as the Netherlands, people even try to claim land back from the sea.

This is the small town of Positano, on the Mediterranean coast of Italy. It is easy to see what an effect storms or a rise in sea level would have.

Hurakan's revenge

The lands of the ancient Maya included the coast of the Yucatan Peninsula of Mexico, as well as coastal regions of present-day Belize and Guatemala. According to Mayan legend, the god of the winds punished humans with terrible storms when he and the other gods were angry. The god's name was Hurakan, and it is said that Spanish explorers named severe storms after him

Hurricane Mitch struck Honduras in 1998. It was a devastating storm that destroyed about 70,000 homes, many near the coast.

(they are called "hurricanes" in English). Today, hurricanes often strike Central America in August and September, causing floods and severe damage to coastal regions.

Bangladesh

The coastline of Bangladesh, in southern Asia, stretches for 360 miles (575 km) along the Bay of Bengal. The land along the coast is flat and easily flooded. The country receives very heavy rain during the **monsoon** season, from mid-May to October. In Bangladesh, tropical storms are called "cyclones," and they often cause disastrous floods. Almost every year, thousands of Bangladeshis lose their homes; in 1998, 25 million were left homeless. Things were made worse by **tsunamis** that swept over the coast.

Bangladesh has a population of 134 million. Those who live near the coast are in great danger of being flooded out of their homes.

Controlling the Coast

The world's coastlines are shaped by the oceans. As waves pound against cliffs, rocks break off and fall to the shore. Moving water then smooths the fallen rocks into smaller pebbles, which are eventually worn down into tiny grains of sand. This process means that shorelines are constantly being worn away, which can make them difficult places to live. For this reason, people have always tried to protect their coastal settlements. In ancient times, they built sea walls and harbors, and very often those defenses lasted for centuries. As the climate changes over long periods of time, however, new forms of protection must be put in place.

▲ *These are the remains of a huge artificial harbor at Caesarea, Israel. It was built around 20 B.C. on the instructions of Herod the Great, King of Judaea, and later taken over by the Romans. The original harbor wall was more than 1,640 feet (500 m) long.*

Sea walls and fences

Sea defenses can protect people living on the coast—but only for a certain time. The sea will always win in the end. Sea walls and **breakwaters** are built to take the force of storm waves. At the foot of cliffs, large piles of boulders or specially shaped pieces of concrete

A sea wall protects the buildings along the seacoast in Havana, Cuba.

can be helpful. The energy of the waves is used up on them so that the cliffs behind feel less force. On beaches, strong wooden fences called groins help break up waves as they crash onto the shore. They also keep sand and pebbles in place. This is important for many people living near the shore, because beautiful seashores bring in tourists, jobs, and income.

Ferry port

Dover, a town on the southeast coast of England, was an important settlement for the ancient Romans, who built a lighthouse there.

Later, the Normans added a castle, and Dover became one of the famous Cinque Ports ("Five Ports"), which provided ships and men for the English king. At the end of the 19th century, Dover gained a new railway station, harbor, and **pier**, which were planned for the first cross-channel rail **ferry** to France. Many people who live in the town today are involved in its life as a working port.

Today, Dover is still an important ferry town, and the harbor and terminal are well protected against the sea.

Reclaiming the Land

People who live in low-lying coastal regions face a constant battle with the sea. In some parts of the world, they build sea walls, **dikes**, and **embankments** to try to win land back from the sea. This is a very difficult process, but there is one region where people have been **reclaiming** land for more than 1,000 years. The Netherlands is one of the Low Countries (along with Belgium and Luxembourg), meaning that much of its land lies below sea level. In ancient times, people built huts on mounds of earth or sand dunes. Then, around the 10th century, they began draining seawater from flooded, swampy areas and building homes there. This process has been going on ever since, and today the Dutch use modern technology to protect their coast.

▲ *Walls of sandbags are sometimes erected in low-lying coastal areas during times of intense flooding to help protect homes and property.*

Polders

The Dutch reclaimed land by building dikes around areas to be drained. Then they used windmills to pump the water into drainage canals. The drained areas are called "polders," and the canals lead to rivers and the North Sea. In 1932, a 20-mile-long (32 km) dike was completed, cutting off a large coastal bay and turning it into a freshwater lake. Much of this lake was then drained to make more polders. The country's lowest polder is 22 feet (6.7 m) below sea level. Today, most Dutch windmills have been replaced by electric pumps.

Storm Surge Barrier

In 1953, huge waves crashed over the dikes and flooded the southern coastal region of the Netherlands, killing more than 1,800 people. In response to this tragedy, the Dutch government decided to build larger, stronger **dams** to close off the mouths of rivers and protect the coast. Engineers worked out a system that would normally allow water to pass through the dam but also enable workers to close it off if there was a very high tide or severe storm. The sea barrier across the East Schelde estuary was opened in 1987. It is 175 feet (53 m) high, and the complete system is 4.2 miles (6.8 km) long.

The Dutch polders make very good farmland, especially for dairy farms, which help produce the country's famous Dutch cheese.

Sixty-two movable steel gates in the barrier can be lowered to keep floodwaters out.

The Frozen North

The Arctic polar region (the frozen area around the North Pole) includes coastlines along three of the world's continents—Asia, North America, and Europe. Since the **climate** is so cold, and the sea is frozen for much of the year, life is hard on the Arctic coast. Yet some people have traditionally made this their home. The Inuit homeland stretches from northeastern Russia, across Alaska and northern Canada, to Greenland. Years ago, most Inuit lived near the coast because the sea provided them with food. They used skin-covered **kayaks** to catch fish and hunt seals. Today, many Inuit have given up this way of life and moved south, but some remain, keeping their culture alive. In 1999, the Inuit officially gained a homeland in Canada when the new northern territory of Nunavut (meaning "Our Land") was created.

A relative of the salmon, fish called char are an important food for Arctic inhabitants, who capture them through the ice.

The name is Nome

The town of Nome, Alaska, lies on the Bering Sea, just below the **Arctic Circle**. It is an important port, though it is generally blocked by

The town of Nome, on the Seward Peninsula coast of Alaska. Some Inuit people still hunt and fish there.

ice from November to May. The town began as an Inuit settlement and grew quickly after gold was discovered nearby in 1899. The town apparently gained its name from a mistake, when a mapmaker misunderstood a query on a previous map that read: "?Name." The population swelled to 20,000, but many disappointed gold-hunters soon left. Today, Nome has about 3,500 people, and the tourist and building industries provide most jobs.

The Chukchi of Siberia

The Chukchi people of northeastern Russia are divided into two groups: the northern group lives on the coast of the East Siberian and Bering seas, while the southern Chukchi are reindeer-herders who live inland. The coastal Chukchi (who are also called Anqallyt, or "sea people") fish and hunt for seals, walruses, and whales. Like the Inuit, they traditionally paddle skin-covered canoes, but today they also drive motorboats and use modern **harpoons**. These "sea people" live in wooden huts in coastal villages and traditionally trade seal skins with the inland Chukchi and their Russian neighbors.

Chukchi people still practice many of their native traditions, including the use of reindeer hides to make clothing.

Tourist Resorts

Many people like to vacation on the coast. They enjoy walking along the cliff tops and admiring the view, relaxing and sunbathing on the beach, and swimming in the sea. Because of this, many coastal villages and towns have been turned into tourist resorts, with plenty of hotels and restaurants. This development began in the 19th century, when the new railways made travel quicker and cheaper. In 1860, for example, British workers started making day-trips to the seaside on their days off. Coastal resorts such as Blackpool and Margate soon developed to meet the new demand. Since then, modern travel packages and escorted tours have encouraged people to travel all over the world on their vacations.

▲ *Myrtle Beach is one of the most famous resorts along the Atlantic coast of South Carolina. There are many hotels and golf courses near the long, wide beach.*

Rimini

In 268 B.C., the Romans built a town called Ariminum on the coast of the Adriatic Sea. Centuries later, the town passed into the control of the Pope. Renamed Rimini, it became part of the kingdom of Italy in 1860 and began to develop as a small seaside resort. One hundred years later, Rimini expanded into one of the biggest beach resorts in Europe. Today, the seafront stretches for nine miles (15 km), and most beaches are lined with restaurants, bars,

It's difficult to imagine now that Rimini was once a quiet seaside town. It is a popular resort because the beaches are well maintained.

and clubs. Some of the beaches are privately owned and charge entrance fees. Many of the 130,000 inhabitants of modern Rimini are involved in tourism.

Goa

The Indian state of Goa has 62 miles (100 km) of tropical coastline along the Arabian Sea. It has been part of India since 1961, but for centuries before that Goa was a Portuguese **colony**. Today, most Goans are Hindus, but many of the people living on the coast are of Portuguese descent and are Christians. The main local food **crop** is rice, and coconuts and fruit are sold in local markets and sent abroad. In recent years, many small resorts have grown up along the beautiful palm-fringed beaches, and vacationers visit Goa from all over the world. Some people are concerned that this has changed the local people's way of life, without bringing them wealth.

A luxury resort in Goa. Unfortunately for the locals, many vacationers stay at their hotel beach and spend little money at local shops and restaurants.

25

Using the Coast

Coasts are a great source of food, entertainment, and adventure. But they are also used as a source of fuel, and much of the world's oil and gas is collected by drilling into the seabed from offshore rigs. Scientists are investigating ways in which wave power and tidal energy could be used to produce electricity. The sea and the ocean floor also contain valuable **minerals**, such as salt. It has been obtained from the world's coasts since ancient times.

Sea salt

Seawater is salty, and when the water evaporates (changes from a liquid to a gas), it leaves the salt behind. This can happen naturally in shallow rock pools beside the sea, if they are left to dry out in hot weather. Industrial salt works are most successful in hot, dry regions of the world. The seawater is allowed to flow into shallow ponds, called pans, which are separated by dikes. As the water evaporates from the pans, the salt is first raked into heaps, and then spread out to dry.

Huge platforms with towers, called derricks, and rigs to operate drilling tools are constructed offshore to explore for gas and oil.

This is hard work, and in industrialized countries, the moving and raking is done by very large machines.

Tidal energy

The world's first tidal power plant opened in 1966 on the coast of Brittany, in northern France. A barrier was built across the estuary of

This salt pan lies off the coast of Sri Lanka, in the Indian Ocean. The heat of the tropical sun evaporates the seawater.

the Rance River, near Saint Malo, where the river flows into the English Channel. There is a difference of up to 44 feet (13.5 m) between high and low tides, and as water flows through the dam, it turns 24 **turbines** that are connected to

electricity **generators**. The turbines can work during incoming and outgoing tides, and fish can pass freely between the sea and the river. As well as being a successful power plant, the Rance dam attracts around 400,000 visitors every year.

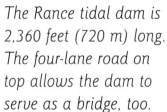
The Rance tidal dam is 2,360 feet (720 m) long. The four-lane road on top allows the dam to serve as a bridge, too.

27

Pollution and Conservation

Most people who live on the coast are careful to look after their environment. They know that any coastline can be damaged easily. Thoughtless people may leave litter on a beach. Factories may pump waste or poisonous chemicals directly into the sea. The governments of many countries now take special steps to care for their coasts and have made strict laws about how their shorelines are used. Some countries have turned parts of their coastlines into national parks, in order to protect them even further. One of the most famous of these is the marine park that surrounds the Great Barrier Reef, just off the coast of northeast Australia.

▲ *This lighthouse lies on the Bay of Fundy, in Canada. The rugged shoreline, which has the highest tides in the world, forms a portion of Fundy National Park.*

Prestige oil disaster

On November 19, 2002, an 800-foot-long (243 m) tanker, the *Prestige*, started leaking oil 125 miles (200 km) off the Galician coast of northwest Spain. The ship then sank, taking a large amount of its 84,700 tons (77,000 t) of oil to the bottom of the Atlantic Ocean. Unfortunately, more oil leaked out, and within days it began washing up on Spanish beaches.

▶

After an oil spill, it is almost impossible to clean the coast completely. This oil came from the sunken tanker Prestige.

More than 560 miles (900 km) of shoreline were affected, many thousands of seabirds were killed, and the coast had to be closed to fishing and shellfish gathering. This affected more than 90,000 local people. Experts believe that this disaster could harm the Galician coast, and nearby shorelines, for up to 20 years.

Welsh national park

The Pembrokeshire Coast National Park, in western Wales, is one of the best protected areas in Europe. The park is most famous for its coastal path, which passes beautiful cliffs, beaches, and inlets. This is also very popular territory for many different kinds of seabirds, including shearwaters and gannets, which means that it attracts thousands of bird-watchers every year. The local people of towns such as Tenby, Pembroke, and St. David's are very proud of the wonderful coast where they live. Nevertheless, there are large **oil refineries** at Milford Haven, just beside the national park, which present constant danger.

COAST PATH

◀

The coastal path in Pembrokeshire, Wales, is almost 190 miles (300 km) long.

Glossary

adapt Change in order to suit the conditions.

Arctic Circle An imaginary circle that stretches around the earth near the northern polar region.

assembly A large meeting.

breakwaters Barriers of boulders or concrete built out into the sea, to protect the coast by breaking up the force of waves.

cape A piece of land that juts out into the sea.

city-state An independent state made up of a city and its surrounding territory.

climate Weather conditions over a long period of time.

colony An area that is ruled by another country.

container A large metal box used for the transportation of goods.

crop A plant grown by people for food.

dams Barriers built to hold back and control the flow of water.

descendants People related to people who lived in the past.

dikes Walls that are built to stop flooding from the sea.

embankments Banks of earth or stone that are built to stop the sea or a river from flooding.

estuary The wide part of a river near its mouth, where it flows into the sea.

ferry A boat that carries passengers.

generators Machines that turn one form of energy, such as the power of water, into electricity.

harpoons Long, pointed pieces of metal or wood used to spear and catch fish.

kayaks A kind of canoe rowed by double-bladed paddles.

minerals Substances that occur naturally in the earth.

monsoon A strong seasonal wind that brings great rain.

oil refineries Industrial plants where impurities are removed from crude oil.

pier A platform built on stilts that juts out into the sea and acts as a landing stage for boats.

ports Places by the sea (or by a river) where boats can dock, load, and unload.

predators Animals that hunt and kill other animals for food.

prehistoric Describing the period before history was recorded in writing.

reclaiming Winning back (land from the sea).

restrictions Rules to limit something (such as overfishing).

sand dunes Mounds or hills of sand formed by the wind.

suburb An outer district at the edge of a city.

tide The rise and fall of sea level, which happens twice a day.

tsunamis Giant sea waves (usually caused by an earthquake).

turbines Machines with blades that are turned by moving water.

31

Index